IDENTITY CRISIS

I0459161

IDENTITY CRISIS

FINDING YOUR IDENTITY IN CHRIST ALONE

MARK GRANT

IDENTITY CRISIS:
Finding Your Identity in Christ Alone

ISBN 978-1-966741-04-6

Mark Grant

Edited by Sheron Wallace

Life Over Coffee
8595 Pelham Rd Ste 400 #406,
Greenville, SC 29615
LifeOverCoffee.com

Your real, new self (which is Christ's and also yours, and yours just because it is His) will not come as long as you are looking for it. It will come when you are looking for Him.

C.S. Lewis, *Mere Christianity*

For additional resources, visit
lifeovercoffee.com

Table of Contents

Introduction

Many of the people we counsel live inside a black hole of self-will, misery, and confusion. They need God to break in on their shadowland from which sin has erased the light of the personal and living God.
—David Powlison

D o you realize that you are the author of your own story? Your response to every season, stage in life, and trial pens a new chapter in your story. For those in Christ, the plot twist to your story is the spiritual awakening experienced by grace: no longer following the course of this world but becoming alive with Christ. Regeneration changes your identity and potential for living well in God's world. However, your new identity often becomes confused from the strain of living life in a fallen world with an indwelling fleshly nature.

Your identity morphs into an unhelpful mixture of Christian and worldly components. Self-reliance is the typical response, leading to useless and sinful counterfeit solutions. Returning to one's new in-Christ identity is a pivotal theme in biblical counseling. Paul's letter to the church in Ephesus is a great example of what this means; the rules for Christian living only come after Paul poetically lays out our new citizenship. This book is not just a theoretical exploration. It aims to help you understand and apply the practical importance of functional identity in a Christian's life.

- Chapter 1 connects your functional identity to your worship.
- Chapter 2 shows how your functional identity can hinder renewed minds.
- Chapter 3 explains how a redemptive life is only possible with an in-Christ identity.
- Chapter 4 clarifies how embracing your real identity can help you persevere in a difficult situation.

I pray this book helps you remember your life is part of God's big story and encourages you to live out each day as a restored image bearer.

Mark Grant

1

Your Thoughts Reveal Functional Identity

Exploring your functional identity during a season of difficulty benefits you in many ways. I'm speaking of your practical life that might conflict with what it means to be a Christian. Wayward hearts and vulnerable souls can easily skew their identities, resulting in the construction of false worship structures, which, when present, can lead to increased hopelessness and difficulty during trials.

Deeper Conversations

Caring for a friend amid a trial is complex. Feelings of inadequacy can surface as one searches for the perfect words to ease the weariness of one's soul. Sympathetic listening is always the ideal starting point, but if soul care is to occur, the conversation must go deeper than superficial discussions. With gentleness and patience, the conversation must lead and encourage them to engage with God to embrace His Sovereign and purposeful work in their lives. God uses all things for their good (Romans

8:28-29), and often, these seasons provide fertile ground to expose idols of the heart and gaps in an individual's gospel understanding.

Due to our fallen natures, we tend to be blind to the things that move us, which are the catalysts that fuel our engines. Even those who are biblically literate often lack a sound grasp of their hearts' ruling motives. One may question the wisdom of this line of reasoning during a season of difficulty. For example, how does directing a wife to understand the idols of her heart help when she is reeling from her husband's recently confessed adultery? This conversation is practically and spiritually profitable from a Christian, gospel-driven perspective.

Suffering wears out the soul, which can be made worse by sin and idolatry (1 Peter 2:11). The purity of your worship directly impacts the health of your soul, and the identification and dismantling of false worship structures (idols of misplaced desires) will help your soul find rest. Heart idols are the fruit of improper thinking, and if this thinking is left unchecked, the conclusions reached amid a season of suffering can lead to further harm by seeking counterfeit solutions. Even amid a life turned upside down, you must remember Christ didn't come to save you from a bad marriage or a lousy job. False worship structures affect our souls by causing us to lose sight of the gospel's good news. In essence, we revert to a works-based salvation, as if Christ's sacrifice isn't sufficient.

Your greatest need remains Christ for your salvation and your ongoing sanctification. As Paul Tripp said, "The good news of the kingdom is not freedom from hardship, suffering, and loss. It is the news of a Redeemer who has come to rescue me from myself. His rescue produces change that fundamentally alters my response to these inescapable realities." Humility positions you to receive Christ's grace (James 4:6). David Powlison states, "Christ powerfully meets people who are aware of their actual need for help. Christ's forte is our acknowledged need in the face of compulsions from within and pressures from without" (2 Corinthians 12:9-10).

- How can you help a friend biblically understand themselves and better respond to their season of suffering?
- How can someone navigate the storylines, emotions, and hurt to help their friend see their heart's tendencies?

One way is to recognize how their worship reflects their identity. Using a person's self-defined identity as an entryway is often effective, helping them ascertain their purpose in life and gain a more accurate assessment of themselves and their environment (Psalm 139:23). This avenue of inquiry can often bring freshness and clarity to their thinking as they focus on the workings of their hearts, ideally leading them to a renewed dependence on Christ for all things (John 15:5). Asking these kinds of questions can help them find rest for their souls and empower forward-moving, hope-filled progress.

> Christian counseling is counseling which exposes our motives—our hearts and our world—in such a way that the authentic gospel is the only possible answer.
>
> —David Powlison

A Christian's True Identity

The Westminster Catechism states that man's chief purpose is to "Glorify God and enjoy Him forever," though sin has taken humanity away from this original position and purpose.

> Individually, we were created to serve God, but sin confused everything, tangling our hearts with pride, false idols, false securities, and false saviors, all knotted together into one disordered mess from which we cannot free ourselves. Only by grace are we given eyes to see the depth of our complex hearts and two-faced motives, and only by grace do we find a Great Physician committed to untangling our disordered hearts.
>
> —Tony Reinke

Hearts are continuously enticed, tempted, and deceived by the lust of the flesh, the lust of the eyes, and the pride of life (1 John 2:16). Hidden and insidious desires always seek to shape lust-filled hearts. You choose things that you perceive as good and desirable, things you think will result in success, comfort, and significance. Over time, these selections metamorphose into your identity.

> How do we make an identity out of temptation? By collapsing what you desire with who you are.
>
> —Rosaria Butterfield

A man may desire to become successful in his career. This desire is okay if he is careful, but if not, he can start placing value on his career. As a result, his career becomes his identity, and his focus turns away from Christ and onto the many opportunities or threats to his career. He has added "career success" to the gospel message. As a result, his joy, or soul health, links to his performance at work, which can manifest many false worship structures. A woman desires to be the perfect mother and starts to define her worth as such. When this happens, her children's public behavior takes on a self-focused commentary, and she becomes fearful about how their actions reflect her parenting ability. Her joy, or soul health, links to something apart from Christ. Again, she has added "perfect mother" to the gospel message.

False identities can even attach themselves to ministry. If a pastor's identity shifts away from Christ to being a pastor, his allegiance will become askew. He will analyze trends in church attendance, the reception of his messages, or the divorce rate of couples he counsels and reach unfortunate conclusions about himself. In all these cases, the individual's thinking turns temporal and their focus inward. Given the wayward tendencies of fallen hearts, the first step you must take daily is to remind yourself of your true identity. During the business of family and work, with all of the entanglements of church and community, you must continue orienting your life to Christ (Colossians 3:11).

> If I may speak my own experience, I find that to keep my eye simply upon Christ, as my peace, and my life, is by far the hardest part of my calling. A thousand such surrenders I have made, and a thousand times I have interpretatively retracted them.
>
> —John Newton

You can see the well-known pastor and hymnist engaged in the conflict we all face as Christians. You want to do right but find yourself doing the opposite (Romans 7:15). It is the daily call to die to yourself (Matthew 16:24).

Understanding the Battle

The fight for your identity is the same flesh-spirit battle you face as a Christian (Galatians 5:17). Using the world's temptations, the enemy aligns with your flesh to shift your identity and, ultimately, your focus away from Christ.

> We should be careful at the temptation to minimize our involvement in taking the bait, for the sinner's rebellious nature finds the forbidden thing more attractive, not because it is inherently attractive, but because it furnishes an opportunity to assert one's self-will.
>
> —John MacArthur

Seeing yourself in the light of truth requires spiritual discernment (Obadiah 1:3) and a firm grasp of the gospel to overcome the indwelling shame, fear, and guilt that reside in your flesh and make it difficult to accept the truth about yourself (John 2:25). The freedom of the gospel only comes when your focus is building up your new identity in Christ and leaving fleshly-inspired identities behind (Philippians 3:13-14). Many Christians never fully reach this point. Their souls are too tender and sensitive from past evil or years of poor care. It is similar to providing care to a burn victim; any attention initially brings pain.

Peeling back the many layers of life's self-centered solutions is too excruciating to allow a new identity to take root (2 Corinthians 5:17). As a result, they stand firm in who they think they are, defending their self-reliant tendencies and self-righteous ways daily. The enticement is the hidden danger of a false identity; it has no power or legitimacy and requires the self to defend, justify, promote, refine, reinvent, and maintain. It creates a heavy yoke and a propensity towards unbelief (Matthew 11:30). Thus, when helping a hurting friend think correctly and biblically about their identity, the disciple must execute with patience, gentleness, and love.

A Final Word

It is essential to state that a properly aligned, in-Christ identity does not eliminate suffering from your life, but it does create a new type of freedom, as evidenced in the life of Apostle Paul. It is clear that his life was full of hardships (2 Corinthians 11:23-29), but he was able to respond positively. For instance, despite being in jail, Paul could see gain (Philippians 1:21), but only because his identity was in the gospel; his joy was Christ's joy. When evil enters your world, it only impacts your temporal life. Your identity in Christ is eternal and remains unchanged, leading you to experience a peace that surpasses your understanding (Philippians 4:7).

To illustrate, I will borrow from Chicken Little's demise. Some of life's difficulties and challenges, represented by rocks of varying shapes and sizes, will fall from the sky and disrupt your existence. If your identity is in something other than Christ, each rock will deliver a crushing blow to you, leaving you dazed and confused. If your identity is in Christ, these rocks will no longer have a crippling effect. Although they still have to be dealt with, you can navigate around the obstacle and address the disruption in a much calmer, gospel-centered, liberating way—in a way that reminds you (and others) that you are a living character in God's wonderful story of redemption.

Call to Action

1. What does it mean to have an identity in Christ?
2. What does having an identity in Christ while living in a fallen body look like?
3. What has a suffering event in your life, whether past or present, revealed about your functional identity in Christ?
4. Why is disappointment a good reminder of where we stand with God?
5. What idol has been in your life that created an identity more valuable than your in-Christ identity? Why did it have an appeal? What will be your next step to repentance if you have not already repented?

2

Change That Annoying Voice in Your Head

What is the controlling voice in your head? I'm talking about the one there before you became a Christian, and it still "talks" to you today. In Ephesians 4:22, Paul explains that the internal dialogue in our minds is part of our old way of life—the "old self"—we carry into our Christian experience. This old self tempts us to seek our identity in achievements, status, or abilities instead of the full worth we have in Christ. Changing our thoughts is a complex process, but there is a way to have the mind of Christ even while existing in a fallen body.

Fatal Attractions

Stacy is a single woman who struggles with her relationships with men. She desires their attention, which can frequently result in impure thoughts, deeds, and disappointment when she learns the source of the attraction is purely sexual. Nick continues to battle his attraction to pornography. Despite turning to Christ in college, getting married, and becoming a father, the pull of this sin seems as strong as ever. Despite exposure to sound gospel teaching, Stacy and Nick struggle in their Christian walk. Each morning starts with hope (Lamentations 3:22-23), but when life's interactions intensify, godly intentions quickly unravel, and they respond like their pre-regenerate selves. Conversations in three areas are needed to help them gain traction against besetting sin:

1. Understanding the Process of Sin
2. Examining Inner Conversations
3. Helping to Simplify Their Identity

The Process of Sin

Most Christians recognize sinful behaviors as the fruit of an evil heart (Luke 6:43-44) but may not fully understand the four-step process described by James.

> But each person is tempted when he is lured and enticed by his own desire. Then desire, when it has conceived, gives birth to sin, and sin, when it is fully grown, brings forth death.
>
> (James 1:14-15)

Step 1: Temptation (Lured)

Part of the human experience is to have a soul that hungers for satisfaction, though we naturally look for delight apart from God (Romans 1:21-23), which is lust or idolatry. As Christians, we are new creations (2 Corinthians 5:17) and have a new Spirit (Ezekiel 36:26-27), but our fallen flesh (Galatians 5:17) remains a magnet for the temptations life brings.

From our individual experiences, rebellious hearts, and fleshly-formed thinking patterns, we each have our particular bent of lust. Usually, it is a self-focused desire or a skewed or perverted variation of God's good gifts of security, intimacy, community, love, sex, et cetera.

Step 2: Enticed By Desire

The next step is the deception of the mind. Once temptation arrives on the scene, a spiritual battle ensues. To complement James's analogy of childbirth, this is when the romancing of the evil act takes place. The promise of satisfaction is highlighted, and the expected consequences are minimized. The bait looks too good to pass up.

Step 3: Conception

Sin conception happens when the fleshly desire captures the believer's heart, and it is only a matter of time before the act follows. At this point, an individual becomes hardhearted, characterized by an inability to discern spiritual reality. Hardened by sin is spiritual blindness at its worst. The hard heart takes action toward the evil desire, and the individual is ready to plunge into sin, apathetic and unmoved by the resulting consequences.

Step 4: Sin

The sin that has been incubating comes to fruition, manifesting its deadly intention.

Stacy and Nick

To help our friends, you must look for ways to break the process of sin before conception. God gives you practical ways to battle temptation in the earliest stages of the process through either limitation or amputation. In essence, this requires radical steps to remove ourselves from situations that present temptations. Limitation is distancing yourself from something, though it might not be a sin, but can be a pathway to sin for you (Hebrews 12:1). Amputation is "plucking out your eye" to radically distance yourself from something (Matthew 5:29-30). The enticement stage is the battle for your mind. As a Christian, you are called to renew your thinking patterns (Ephesians 4:22-23, 2 Corinthians 10:5, Philippians 4:8), but what does this practically look like, and how does correct thinking incapacitate the process of sin? To find the answer, you must explore the role of your internal conversation.

The Running Commentary

I am talking about the conversation in your head that never seems to run out of things to say. I don't fully understand this conversation, but I suspect it is a mixture of your will (desires), conscience (Romans 2:15), and knowledge as they are contoured, influenced, and shaped by the Spirit. In addition to contributions from the Spirit (John 14:26), there are possibly demonic forces seeking to manipulate and incline your will one way or another (Genesis 3:1). This conversation combines facts and opinions. In many ways, it resembles a TV talk show or broadcast of a sporting event.

I describe the dialogue as a mere conversation between two voices: one presenting the facts or asking questions, and the other providing commentary and analysis about the subject or event. I will refer to the first voice as the play-by-play announcer (PBPA) and the latter as the color commentator (CC). Usually, the PBPA voice is fine for a Christian. Spiritual enlightenment (1 Corinthians 2:12-14) has occurred, and a scripturally well-informed PBPA voice can provide biblical insight into the "live-streamed" events of our lives. The voice that gives most Christians problems is the CC, where the mind deceives you. If left unchecked, the CC often works to get your mind off Christ and onto self-sufficient and, usually, sinful solutions to gain satisfaction.

Stacy's Commentator

- PBPA: Stopping to get some coffee. Look, a nice-looking man is working behind the counter.
- CC: I wonder if he thinks I am cute? Let's see if he

gives me that second look. Come on, check me out.
- PBPA: Nope. He is now helping another female customer with "big curves."
- CC: What makes me think he would check me out? I don't have the body guys want. I will never be loved.

Here, the CC romanced Stacy with the bait of male attention. She wants to be an attractive, desirable woman worthy of being noticed by the opposite sex. She wants to be accepted, protected, and loved by a man. In her Adamic brokenness, her thinking and past gains connect to her physical beauty and sex. This disappointment can tempt her toward sexual lust.

Nick's Commentator

- PBPA: I didn't get the promotion.
- CC: That is so unfair! So much for the Disney vacation or helping with the church building project.
- PBPA: Your coworkers Carol and Diana are walking up ahead. Remember, lusting is a sin.
- CC: I deserve a little pick-me-up. How can I not check out those curves? So which one do I think is more attractive? What if they were both wearing bikinis?

Again, the CC was able to shift Nick's focus to worldly things and to arouse sexual desires. He wants to be a successful manager, an admired father, and a godly husband. In short, he wants to be good at everything he values. In his Adamic brokenness, his past gains relate to his school performance and gaining attention from females. This event feeds his flesh (Galatians 6:8) and lures him to respond to the job disappointment by escaping into his fantasy world.

These conversations are silly, but they help illustrate

how internal discussions can remain worldly. The dialogue remains unregenerate, and the old nemeses of legalism, self-sufficiency, and self-righteousness enter into the conversation more or less undetected. Redeemed thinking requires more than biblical knowledge. Most of the time, it mandates you to fire your color commentator!

Commentators and Fruit Identity

Drawing from chapter one, you recall how your desires metamorphose into your identity. Stacy and Nick's identity was not in Christ but a complex mix of the many micro-identities rooted in self. Additionally, you see a connection between their identity and the internal commentary of their CC. What captures the interest and concern of their CC is their purpose and position, namely their identity. Your interpretations of the events in your life depend on your goal and what you believe you deserve. As a result, your internal commentary becomes clouded by the alliance to your false identities (Ephesians 4:17). An unchecked CC is the Achilles heel of your internal conversation, leading you away from simply resting in Christ.

> Thou knowest thou hast formed me with passions wild and strong, and listening to their witching voice has often led me wrong.
>
> —Robert Burns

For Stacy and Nick to gain traction in their Christian lives, they must recognize and shed their many false competing identities and simply find rest in their new Christ identity. This lasting change will only occur with the employment of a new Color Commentator.

A Better Color Commentator

One of the more substantial blessings of regeneration is the indwelling presence of the Holy Spirit. Through this beautiful union, clouded in mystery, you now have the mind of Christ (1 Corinthians 2:15-16), which is the CC you need to put into play. It doesn't come without a considerable investment of time and effort. You cannot know God's mind unless you have His heart and Spirit and share in His character. Your task is for the character of Christ to transform your CC through Scripture reading, memorization, and prayer. To change your CC's character, you must recognize the waywardness of everything about you, stripping away the deceptive workings of the flesh until only your in-Christ identity remains (Matthew 5:3). Careful, honest gospel self-examination of your functional identity should bring you to recognize, "I am more broken than I ever imagined, which exposes a troubling level of depravity in my heart and creates in me a desperate dependence on Christ." In this context, reading the Bible, meditating, memorizing Scripture, and praying can profoundly transform the character of your CC.

Gospel Simplicity

As a Christian, you are in the lifelong battle of seeing past the workings of your flesh, counting all gains as a loss (Philippians 3:7-9), and becoming more humble in your own eyes, more weaned from self, more fixed on Him as your all-in-all. Gospel simplicity is the only way to find freedom from the trappings of the flesh. Suppose Stacy and Nick successfully strip away the areas of spiritual complexity formed by the many self-created micro-identities in their lives. In that case, their newly created CC will result in new freedom in life.

Stacy's CC can quickly remind her of the genuine acceptance and love from Christ and enable her to acknowledge her counterfeit, unsatisfying, and destructive desires for male attention. She is now free to look around the coffee shop and find another single woman who looks like they could use a friend.

With news of the promotion, Nick can decisively find comfort in God's flawlessly ordained plan. His biblically informed, gospel-motivated CC reminds him that God withholds no good thing (Psalm 84:11), so his focus can turn outward, endeavoring to serve his coworkers selflessly.

Call to Action

1. How did your color commentary sound before becoming a Christian?
2. How has your Christianity impacted your internal conversation?
3. What is one area where your in-Christ identity still does not rule your color commentary?
4. What is your practical plan to change this so you can mature into your in-Christ identity?

3

Turn Arguments Into Redemptive Communication

Couples facing marriage difficulties often point to poor communication as the core issue. However, much of the conflict arises from each partner's pursuit of functional identities—seeking fulfillment in roles, status, or personal achievements apart from Christ. Despite a desire for change, old interaction patterns resurface, especially in moments of conflict. True hope for transformation comes when these patterns shift, allowing arguments to become opportunities for redemptive communication.

Communication Problems

Sue and Ken are struggling; their marriage is tense and stressful. They have sought counsel from their church many times but have found little lasting change. It took them a lot of work to define the source of the problem, which is usually described as a communication issue. Recently, Sue was encouraged by Ken's desire to attend a small group at church, hoping this community would help transform their marriage. Unfortunately, it all unraveled after Ken belittled Sue's cooking in front of the group.

Ken complimented the food prepared by the hosts and shared, "Maybe you can give Sue some cooking lessons. She burned the dinner so badly last night that the dog didn't eat it." Sue was hurt and defensive, "I was busy taking care of four kids, doing laundry, and trying to cook dinner. I lost track of time. If only I could get some help from my husband, maybe I would be a better cook!" The ugliness of their marriage was on full display. On the way home, Ken said he was never going back. The hope of the small group being the answer to their marriage problems was gone. Sue was heartbroken and sought help.

- How should the gospel impact a couple's interactions in the heat of conflict?
- What must Sue know to help her navigate this situation without feeling like a doormat?

Sue's Identities

Sue's response was typical and expected. Her explanation was accurate when she said Ken was not a servant leader. Additionally, his poor soul care left her defensive and fragile. She was hurt and embarrassed. But her response employed worldly wisdom and was not beneficial to their marriage. She resorted to rhetorical strategies, almost thinking they would persuade Ken to agree with her assessment of his poor husbandry. Ken's heart is hard, and progress will only come with repentance. Thus, Sue must align herself with God's ways (Romans 2:4) to help him. To help her get there, she needs to understand the role of her identity in her response.

When I speak of identity, I refer to one's purpose and position, i.e., how does she see herself? Individuals typically do not consciously think about their identity. It is one of those areas where you can drift into an auto-pilot mode. For instance, men can find their identity in their careers and women in their relationships (wife/mother). At first glance, these identities seem harmless, but they put you on the wrong path. Christians identify themselves in two main categories: in Christ or something apart from Christ. Sue's real identity is in Christ. God regenerated her and filled her heart with the Holy Spirit. She is an adopted child of God and a fellow heir with Christ (Romans 8:17). This new position brings a new purpose: "to glorify God and enjoy Him forever."

Sue's desire to be a godly wife whom her husband loves became her functional identity that night. It morphed into an object of worship, which was the purpose of attending the small group. When you place your identity in something other than Christ, you position yourself to respond in self-reliant and self-righteous ways to protect and defend your purpose and plans. Sue was ready to react naturally to this functional identity before Ken spoke cruelly. The mind map below shows how this plays out. Despite attempting to protect herself, the response resulted in a restless soul. Going through the different nodes, you see several traits that make up her functional identity.

Functional Identity

- **SPIRITUAL PRIDE:** You can forget your total dependence on God for everything and trust in your intuition to get through life. In this case, Sue wanted to be in control, and the desire for love from her husband (a good thing) elevated to a point where his actions controlled her (fear of man), setting her up to be a sinning victim. When sinfully attacked, Sue responded by becoming hurt and angry. She was spiritually proud, and the Holy Spirit was not leading her. She was not modeling grace. Sue was operating out of the flesh (with all its associated desires), and as a result, it produced the fruits of the flesh (Galatians 5:16-24).

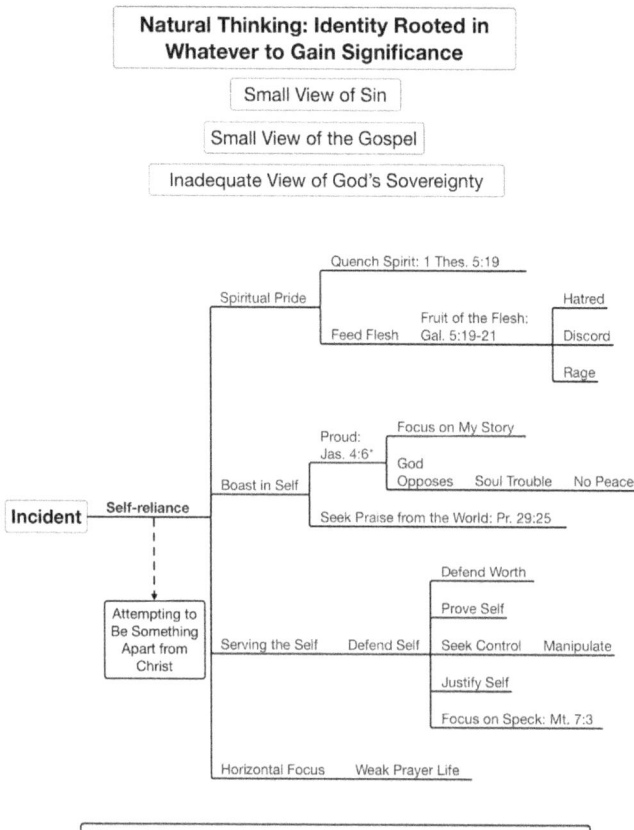

Natural Thinking: Identity Rooted in Whatever to Gain Significance

Small View of Sin

Small View of the Gospel

Inadequate View of God's Sovereignty

Incident — Self-reliance — Attempting to Be Something Apart from Christ

Spiritual Pride
- Quench Spirit: 1 Thes. 5:19
- Feed Flesh — Fruit of the Flesh: Gal. 5:19-21 — Hatred, Discord, Rage

Boast in Self
- Proud: Jas. 4:6* — Focus on My Story; God Opposes — Soul Trouble — No Peace
- Seek Praise from the World: Pr. 29:25

Serving the Self — Defend Self
- Defend Worth
- Prove Self
- Seek Control — Manipulate
- Justify Self
- Focus on Speck: Mt. 7:3

Horizontal Focus — Weak Prayer Life

Proud: *Failure to accept the reality of utter dependence on God, a peculiar kind of insanity caused by a lack of humility.*

- **BOAST IN SELF:** When you take the self-sufficient posture, you must continually deal with indwelling guilt and shame by puffing yourself up. You desperately want people to see that you are good. You want them to understand your motives, no matter how poorly your actions become. Your eyes become fixed on your story. You become downcast and fearful if things are not going according to your script. Consequently, because you have not humbled yourself under a sovereign God, you position yourself against God (James 4:6).

- **SERVING THE SELF:** When operating from a self-sufficient perspective, you protect yourself at all costs, whereby you naturally take the defensive posture; you justify actions, you argue your case, and you seek to gain control of the direction of the conversation or situation. Manipulating techniques, such as anger, come into play (James 4:1-3).

- **HORIZONTAL FOCUS:** A natural consequence of self-sufficiency is that God becomes distant, and your focus shifts to other people. Your prayer life becomes lifeless and anemic, and God seems distant. Due to her functional identity, Sue took a self-protecting posture. She defended her actions and shared her insight on the actual problem. Sue must change her methods and fight redemptively to help Ken move toward a humble, others-centered position.

A Redemptive Posture

Redemptive thinking requires an in-Christ identity and maintaining a singular focus on Christ. It requires a firm grasp of the theology of sin, knowledge and appropriation of gospel application, and the ability to trust God's sovereign hand. This different path, illustrated in this mind map, shows how Sue can answer with a faith-fueled response rooted in grace.

When sin presents itself, the tendency is to become angry (Ephesians 4:26), but instead of reacting to defend herself, she must use this energy redemptively. Her temptation to selfishly react will be out of the way, allowing the Holy Spirit to lead her. She will appropriate a correct view of her dependence on God and realize she can do nothing apart from Christ (John 15:5), which leads to a redemptive posture. Note the following in-Christ realities.

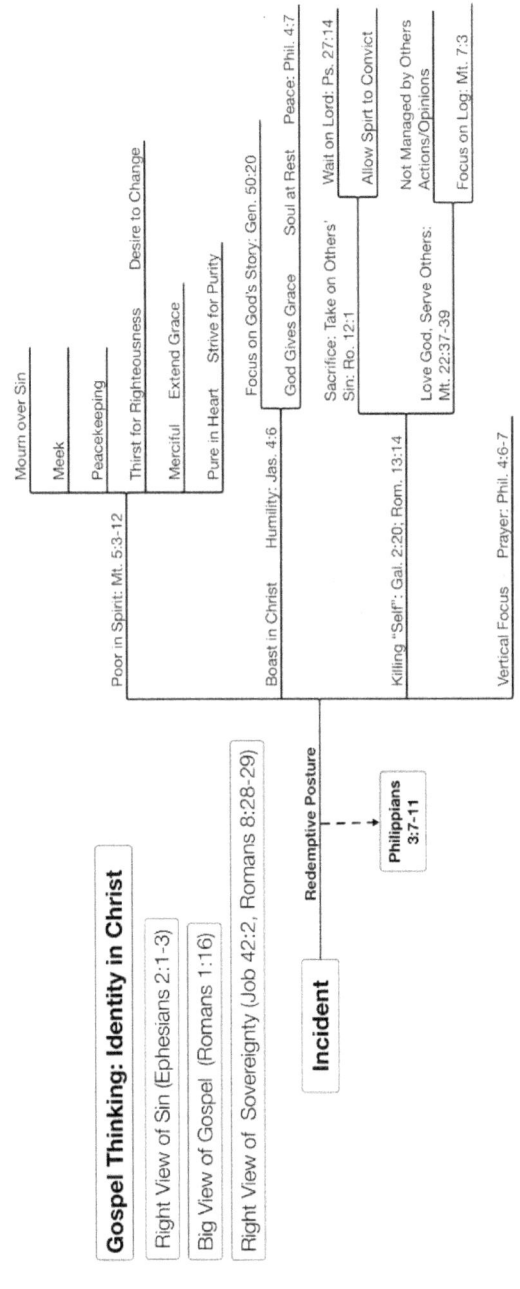

- **POOR IN SPIRIT:** Since Sue recognizes her spiritual bankruptcy, the Holy Spirit will illuminate her mind. Mourning over her sin will lead to humility, a desire for relational restoration (peacemaker), and a thirst for righteousness. She will see the goodness of God's righteousness and desire to manifest His will on earth and in her life, precipitating acts of mercy and a striving for personal holiness.
- **BOAST IN CHRIST:** With her new purpose—bringing glory to God—and correct position—servant of the King—Sue will take a humble posture focusing on God's story. Her soul will find rest through receiving God's grace.
- **THE KILLING OF SELF:** With the flesh out of the way, Sue is positioned correctly for the pivotal point in this process: a willingness to "take on his sin" until it can be dealt with at the cross in God's perfect timing; it is an act of sovereign and undeserved grace.

With her identity firmly rooted in Christ, she is now free to respond from a position of self-sacrifice, love, and forgiveness, enabling her to react graciously, mercifully, and without taking offense. Sue could have simply said, "Yeah, the meal was pretty bad," and allowed the evening to continue and small group gospel relationships to form. As she waits for the Lord's leading, Sue can decide whether to discuss this event later or let love cover Ken's sin.

Final Thoughts

Unequivocally, this is the more challenging but higher road; it is the dying-to-yourself road. Taking a natural way, defending her position, and expecting him to care about her feelings will only result in further ongoing relational deterioration, animosity, and increasing dysfunctional communication. Taking the humble road is the best way to travel. It is the path that most accurately reflects the life of Christ and demonstrates an unrelenting and steadfast trust in the Holy Spirit's ability to penetrate, soften, and transform the hearts of those who sin against you. Seeking contentment in your Heavenly Father as Christ did takes the stress, strain, and expectations off of imperfect, bound-to-fail human relationships.

This type of response redirects them to the only One who can fulfill them—Christ. For too many Christians, this approach seems upside down, but that is the nature of the gospel. God's anger is always redemptive and requires great sacrifice. The gospel gives you opportunities to help spread His kingdom on earth, but it requires you to do the same. Sometimes, you must be quiet, commit it to God, and keep serving the immature and self-centered sinners. With the Spirit's leading, you will love your spouse well, and as God gives growth, you will move towards enjoying the benefits of having a spouse with a well-cared-for soul. To restore their marriage, Ken and Sue must look to enjoy their marriage relationship in the context of a child of God first and foremost. Their worship structures are corrected, which positions them to take redemptive postures when interacting.

Call to Action

1. How challenging is it to respond in Christlike ways when someone sins against you? Perhaps discussing this tension with your spouse or a friend would prove beneficial.
2. Describe a situation when you were the victim/sinner. Why is this construct common, and what did you learn from your situation?
3. How can a person truly be born again, yet have a functional identity that is different from their

regeneration identity?

4.   Based on this chapter, how would you counsel Sue? Sharing your thoughts with a friend would be an excellent life over coffee conversation.

DISCLAIMER: *I am not saying this is appropriate for all marriage discord. If abuse is present, please take steps to prevent physical harm. Your church elders and local law officials may need to intervene. The context for the redemptive posture discussed in this chapter is for couples who are struggling with their communication where abuse is not present.*

4

How to Bring the Gospel of Hope to a Bad Marriage

An unchanging spouse can complicate any marriage, especially when you want your spouse to change so badly that you use sin to make it happen. The Bible presents an alternative path: the gospel of hope. However, this hope comes through sacrifice and learning to uphold our identity rooted in Christ. Learning how to bring the gospel to bear on a bad marriage is life-giving, Christ-exalting, and practically rewarding for any couple.

Internal and External

He hurts, crushes, and destroys my hope at every turn. I'm dying a slow soul death, drowning in hopelessness and negativity. I intensely, desperately want to escape this prison of pain, fear, insecurity, loneliness, and there is a lack of intimacy that holds me captive. Simultaneously, I feel a sense of extreme pity and sorrow for this hollow shell of a man, and I realize I must extend to him the same kindness,

*love, mercy, and forgiveness the Lord has shown
me, even when I have been at my worst.*

—Counselee

These counseling situations weigh heavy on a counselor's soul. God may or may not grant repentance for the husband (2 Timothy 2:25), and the local church is often unable or ill-equipped to engage him or minister to his soul. She has no shepherd. How can the gospel soften and transform this problematic situation? (See Titus 3:4-6, Romans 2:4, Colossians 3:12, Ephesians 4:30-32, Galatians 5:6.) To help organize your thoughts, I have two mind maps:

1. An internal plan to nurture her soul.
2. An external plan to cooperate with the Lord
    in creating an environment to minister to her
    husband's soul, hoping to lead him toward
    repentance and growth.

Major Marriage Mess

Although each story differs, I have observed four fundamental themes providing context for this all-too-common marriage dynamic. (This discussion assumes that the husband and wife are both Christians.) The gospel is shining brighter in the woman than in her spouse. God has opened her spiritual eyes, and her grasp of the gospel and desire to follow Christ is greater than that of her husband. Her in-Christ identity drifts. Healthy wishes of love and marriage often elevate to idolatrous levels, and over time, these controlling desires commingle with the wife's identity. The health of her soul becomes dependent on the health of her marriage.

God's design is for the husband to care for the wife's soul, but the headwaters of soul care is not always Christ. The husband is gospel-immature and will turn to passive or aggressive self-reliant responses as he reacts to the fallenness in his life. When passive, he shrinks back from his God-given responsibilities through withdrawal or blame-shifting. He occupies his time with distracting activities such as sports, career, or video games. Other times, he takes an aggressive approach in an attempt to restore his internal peace by regaining control through anger and manipulation.

Steps to isolate his wife also come into play. He may use the trappings of legalism to gain control, evoking shame and fear through scripture passages like Ephesians 5:22. Some husbands become master manipulators. The wife and the husband have a history of poor soul care predating marriage. There are additional negative consequences of not being raised by godly fathers (Ephesians 6:4). The wife's father, coupled with past opposite-sex relationships, did not minister to her soul, which often elevates her desires for male love and affection to idolatrous levels. The husband's father did not provide a good model of soul care to his wife, leaving the son to learn from the world's teaching. He may know how to provide for her physically, but not spiritually.

Gospel Gameplan

The gospel can improve the situation, but you must understand change first. Our Adamic natures are potentially unchangeable. The Holy Spirit can transform hearts, but we are all works in progress, and fleshly temptations linger. Often, sanctification is slow. The primary goal must not be to change the husband's behaviors; it must be personal growth in worship and service, which leads to a restful soul. The wife seeks to develop two game plans: institute a plan to nurture her soul (internal) and then look to help her husband (external). The first mind map below outlines the plan. To start this journey, she must expand her thinking to include God. She cannot receive God's grace or minister to her husband until she has wrestled with God.

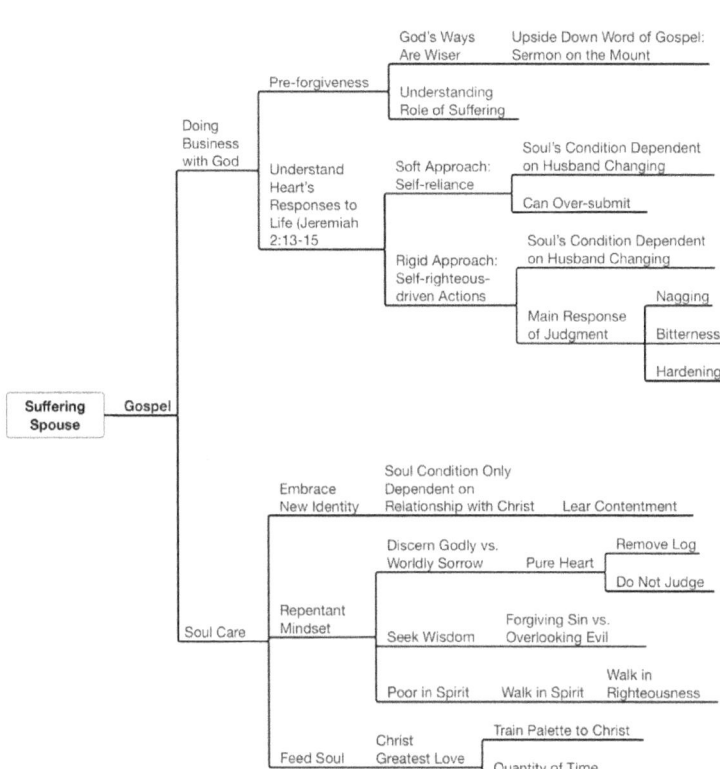

Internal Game Plan for a Problem Marriage

This step is crucial because it gives her time to perceive the Lord's mind about what happened to her as much as she can perceive it. She must establish a theologically precise view of God in her mind, which means He has convinced her that He is working for her good in ways she did not expect and had not perceived up to this point. She also needs to gain a gospel view of suffering and an understanding of her heart to realize how the nemeses of self-sufficiency and self-righteousness affect her responses to this challenging situation.

Often, a wife will take a soft approach by placing the burden of change on herself, believing her shortcomings as a godly wife are to blame for her husband's actions. Her indwelling shame can lead her to over-submit and not confront evil, leaving the husband in sin (Galatians 6:1). Other times; a wife can fall into a legalist, self-righteous mindset and begin to judge her husband's behaviors; she becomes the moral police. If the husband does not change, the wife will become frustrated and head down the path of cynicism and bitterness. Roots of unbelief can grow, leaving her vulnerable to fleshly temptations.

The common error in both approaches is the wife's belief that her happiness or soul health depends on her husband's actions or love. If the husband cannot serve as a godly leader, the wife must repent of her idolatry and find other sources of Christ's grace. This change in her mind is the key to her survival.

> Experiencing the full life with Jesus, we say with David, "You have put more joy in my heart than they have when their grain and wine abound" (Psalm 4:7). We can be infinitely and enduringly happier with Jesus than with anything or even everything in a world without Him.
>
> —Marshall Segal

There are three areas of focus for soul care.

First, the wife must embrace her new identity as a daughter of God. The thoughts of being unlovable, unworthy, etc., must be replaced with her true identity in Christ (Romans 8:17). Once she understands all she has in Christ, she can learn to be content in all circumstances (Philippians 4:11-13). Her soul's health improves as she detaches from her physical environment.

Secondly, through daily meditation on the gospel, the wife must learn how to put on a repentant mindset. She must enter through the gate of spiritual bankruptcy to walk in the Spirit. Poor in Spirit leads to mourning, meekness (humility), and a thirst for righteousness (Matthew 5:3-6). Now, her heart will start to have a change in desires. The focus is no longer on herself but on living out her new identity in Christ. She will extend mercy, seek purity, and extend peace (Matthew 5:7-10). As she understands her heart, her ability to discern Godly sorrow from worldly sorrow will increase, allowing her to seek God's wisdom. She will know when to let love overlook sin (1 Peter 4:8) and when to speak into her husband's life to confront evil.

Thirdly, she must consider how God uses this season to refine her taste for Christ. The wife's flesh can train her tastes to satisfy the world's junk food. She can place her hope in marriage, sex, health, wealth, looks, and other things that can't hold water (Jeremiah 2:13). She must lean into Christ through reading the Word, prayer, worship, fellowship, church, and service. Sometimes, fellowship with the Lord will be sweet, and other times dry, but she must continue to seek biblical paths (Jeremiah 29:13). As Tim Keller said, "Quality time with the Lord is obtained by quantity." As Christ's grace feeds her soul, she will feel like she has a rudder to maneuver through the storm. The wife is now in a position to help her husband.

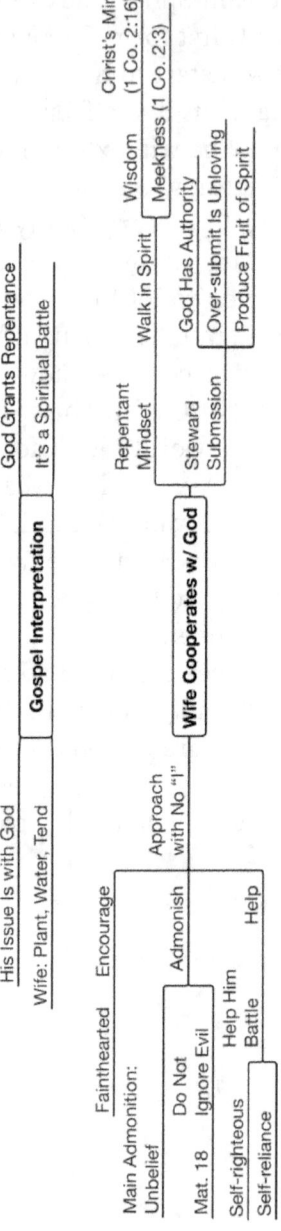

Soul Care for Your Spouse

His Issue Is with God

God Grants Repentance

Wife: Plant, Water, Tend

Gospel Interpretation

It's a Spiritual Battle

Main Admonition:
Unbelief

Faithearted   Encourage

Approach
with No "I"

Admonish

Mat. 18

Do Not
Ignore Evil

Help Him
Battle

Help

Self-righteous

Self-reliance

Wife Cooperates w/ God

Repentant
Mindset

Walk in Spirit

Steward
Submsssion

God Has Authority

Over-submit Is Unloving

Produce Fruit of Spirit

Wisdom

Meekness (1 Co. 2:3)

Christ's Mind
(1 Co. 2:16)

External Game Plan

To serve as a helper to her husband, she must view her husband through the gospel while looking to cooperate with God, as shown in the mind map above. When he struggles to love his wife as Christ, she must remember the spiritual conflict in the context of Christian life. The indwelling sinful nature rebels against God's authority, and His enemies tempt him to doubt God's goodness. He struggles more with his relationship with God than with his wife. Her actions can help or hinder, but she is not capable or responsible for his change. Her call is to plant, water, and tend (1 Corinthians 3:6). Second, she must pray for spiritual discernment to determine if her husband is faint-hearted, weak, or idle (1 Thessalonians 5:14).

- If discouraged, look to encourage.
- If weak, look for ways to help him battle his natural tendency of self-righteousness and self-sufficiency.
- If idle, admonish in humility (Matthew 7:1-5). The fleshly motivation methods of shame, threats, and fear hold no value in God's economy.

Remember, Christ's main admonishment to His disciples was calling out their unbelief (Matthew 8:26, 14:31, 16:8). The husband's most significant issue is unbelief, which prevents him from moving forward in God's call on his life. The wife must look to steward her submission to help him overcome his unbelief. If he is in sin and unwilling to repent, she must follow the example of Matthew 18:15-20 and seek help from church elders to help him grow into his future glory-self. Outside counsel can sometimes help if he is willing to listen. She must continually seek prayer and counsel from others to bring God's glory and produce the fruit of the Spirit (Galatians 5:22-23).

Summary

How can you keep your focus on your in-Christ identity when life becomes difficult? He is the source of living water (John 4:14) and the cornerstone (Ephesians 2:20). Who are the godly men or women in your church who can come alongside you during this season? Become a local church member and intentionally engage that body; let that community serve you. Remember that your flesh and the world continuously highlight the joy of romance and marriage. The gospel teaches something different.

> *I am never going to have paradise in my marriage. Paradise is to come. I am never married to a perfect person. That person will never be my Messiah. The person I am married to has no capacity whatsoever to change my heart. That person I am married to has no capacity whatsoever to bring satisfaction and contentment to my heart. They have no ability whatsoever to deliver me from my sin. They just have no ability to do any of that.*
>
> – Paul Tripp

I pray as you tap into Christ's grace that your soul finds rest, peace enters, and you find joy in worshiping and serving the Lord—always looking for where He is working.

Call to Action

1. Will you share the internal game plan mindmap with a friend and discuss the various aspects, applying them to your life? Ideally, it would be best for a husband and wife to discuss this mindmap together.

2. Will you share the external game plan mind map with a friend, discuss the various aspects, and apply them to your life? Again, it would be ideal for a husband and wife to discuss this mindmap together.

Epilogue

I hope these chapters provide clarity on how examining one's identity is an essential starting point for counseling yourself and others. When we dig deeper, we begin to see how our *functional* identity—what we live out in daily life—reflects what we genuinely value. This self-examination reveals what we believe is right or righteous. And when you begin to talk about righteousness or justification, you are stepping directly into the heart of the gospel.

The core issue is unbelief. As Christians, even though we have been justified by Christ, we can fall into doubt, slipping back into a works-based righteousness. Richard Loveless rightly observed, "Only a fraction of the present body of professing Christians are solidly appropriating the justifying work of Christ in their lives. In their day-to-day existence, they rely on their sanctification for justification."

This points to a critical truth: we must continually remind ourselves of the gospel, letting it shape our hearts, actions, and relationships. The gospel does more than inform our beliefs; it *transforms* how we live. Whenever we act as if the gospel isn't enough, we will seek our validation in other places—whether in power, rebellion, acceptance, or something else. At the root of these sins is a failure to fully trust that Christ's finished work is sufficient. We try to justify or beautify ourselves apart from Him.

Our persistent struggles with sin are a sign that we have lost sight of our complete acceptance in Christ. Like Paul urged the Galatians, we must continually remind ourselves of the gospel's power. When we walk in line with the truth of the gospel, it transforms not just our beliefs but also our behaviors and relationships. The gospel is the only path to true freedom and lasting hope.

To dig deeper into how the gospel transforms every area of life, I encourage you to explore the many resources available at Life Over Coffee. You'll find helpful insights in podcasts, articles, and videos on topics such as gospel-centered identity, sanctification, and the importance of self-counsel, all aimed at equipping you to live out the transformative power of Christ in your daily life.

Your brother in Christ,

Mark

About the Author

Mark Grant graduated from our Mastermind Program and continues training and writing for our ministry here at Life Over Coffee. He is an Engineer, obtaining his Master's degree from the Ohio State University, and works for the Navy as a civilian engineer. With his marriage healed after finding Christ, his passion increased to help others apply the gospel to everyday life. He continues to be amazed at God's sufficient counsel through the Word and the work of the Spirit. He is married to Lesa and the thankful father of his daughter Aislinn. He cheers for his Buckeyes, takes on various home projects, and has a glass kiln to try his hand at making fused glass landscapes. Mark is an excellent cook, too.

Other Books Available from
Life Over Coffee

www.ingramcontent.com/pod-product-compliance
Lightning Source LLC
Chambersburg PA
CBHW071545120626
46550CB00006B/2589